MY STORY

THE EARLY YEARS

A Story of Life

Eldridge David Gibbs Jr.

ISBN 978-1-0980-3188-6 (paperback)
ISBN 978-1-0980-3189-3 (digital)

Christian Faith Publishing, Inc.
832 Park Avenue
Meadville, PA 16335
www.christianfaithpublishing.com

Printed in the United States of America

CONTENTS

INTRODUCTION

At this late hour of my life at the age of eighty, I have felt, not only the urge to write about part of my life, but in some ways, it seemed a necessity. It is not intended to be a history or an awe-inspiring biography of my life. In many ways, I do not feel that I intend it to place a spotlight on me at all. It is intended primarily for some future generations who may find this (perhaps some not even born at this writing), dust it off, and read about life. I feel that this could be a worthwhile endeavor for most of us in our latter years, and I highly recommend it, regardless of one's writing skills. I would just hope that if several of my descendants do read this someday, perhaps one might say, "I'm glad he wrote that, and I'm glad that I read it."

I would like to thank those who were part of my life, so that I might be able to remember them and write of some of the events they shared or inspired. I thank Deanna, my beautiful, patient wife of thirty-nine years at this writing for tolerating an excessive amount of my time on the computer. I especially thank Dee since she was not in this part of my life, but thank God, she is now. I also must thank God Almighty for even allowing me to recall these memories at my age, and being able to assemble them into this little book, even if the publishers might find no merit or value to publish it.

CHAPTER ONE

LIFE ON JENKINS STREET

IN THE BEGINNING

I know that I was likely conceived between Thanksgiving and Christmas of 1937, since I was born September 26, 1938. Mom always said I was late. She may have been right. I weighed in at ten pounds, twelve ounces. That is obviously quite large, and she always said that I had a rather peculiar blue color. I think I recall that she also said I peeled some later. At any rate, I first appeared into this world in a second floor home on Jenkins Street in Richmond County, Augusta, Georgia. At this writing, I am not absolutely sure of the address, but there were only two each two-story dwellings on Jenkins Street, and they both still stand today. I think I know which one, but I'm not sure, and since I'm not famous, it's really not that important, and I've probably spent too much time with it already.

I had a much-loved first cousin, Alice Reeves, who was born in June before I arrived in September. Alice was the first-born to Mom's older brother, Uncle William Homer "Willie" Reeves and Aunt Montine (Peppers), and in fact, Alice was an only child until we were both early teens. Maybe we'll have more about that another time. Where I was going with this was, that Mom was rather short; about 5'2" while Aunt Montine was probably taller than the average lady (around 5'6" or 5'7"). Whether I was late or not, Mom got pretty big while carrying me. She always said she never really saw her feet for about six months. Aunt Montine, however, was one who hardly showed, plus she was taller and a little "lanky." Even though she carried Alice to full term, she still weighed only a little more than five pounds. I suppose I digressed (probably too much) to get to this little story. Mom said that when she was only about three months along, she was already looking quite pregnant, while Aunt Montine, who was now about six months along hardly showed at all—just a little "pooch." Anyway, Mom went to the doctor with Aunt Montine. When the nurse came out, she walked toward Mom (probably offering to help her out of her chair) and said, "Hello, Mrs. Reeves, let me help you come with me to see the doctor." She didn't even look toward Aunt Montine at that time, and it was her appointment.

I was told that my parents shared the house on Jenkins Street with one of Mom's older sisters, Aunt Eleanor and Uncle Bill Holden along with Uncle Willie and Aunt Montine and, of course, Alice. Mom and Dad and my older sister, Nancy, lived upstairs. When my arrival time was approaching, Mom was upstairs and began to have hard labor pains. Of course, there were no cell phones back then, and most folks didn't even have phones in their homes. Since all three families were "poor folks," that was the case. University Hospital was Augusta's City hospital in those days (long before Augusta became the medical center that it is today, at this writing). I don't know every detail, but someone, perhaps Dad, went for help, hoping to find Mom's doctor. The hospital was in the general vicinity, but it was a long walk (or run) for Dad or someone. Upon arriving at the hospital, it was learned that the doctor was unavailable, and they would attempt to locate him while two interns would respond to (1) deliver the baby (me), or to (2) witness the activity, (3) take notes, and (4) learn how it was done. I was told that when they arrived breathlessly up the stairs, I was pretty much on the scene, Mom had badly bent the metal headboard of the iron bed frame where she birthed me. The two interns mostly had to clean things up a bit, try and make Mom more comfortable, and while they were starting to clean me up, the doctor arrived, congratulating those two future doctors on performing so well! Mom said I then "peed" in his face (not on purpose, though; I like doctors).

I really don't recall much about residing in my place of birth on Jenkins Street. I don't know why, since I've always felt I had a pretty good memory. Perhaps it was because I was so young. There were probably lots of cute stories, and I am sure you would have enjoyed them.

THE HAIRCUT STORY

I do recall this story that I was told. Aunt Eleanor and Uncle Bill had two wonderful sons; Billy (at least Billy back then; he later became Bill around the time he was later becoming an outstanding dentist). Billy (or Dr. Bill) was about a year older than my sister, Nancy (age three), who was near the same age as his younger brother, Jimmy. The story goes (at least as I recall) that the three of them had a neighborhood friend (I don't recall her name. It may have been Roslyn) that they spent a good bit of time with. Well, one fine day, she decided it might be a good time for her to give them haircuts, and at no charge! This seemed to the three of them to be a terrific idea, and they saw no reason to ask for references for her experience in this hair-care field since they felt they already knew her quite well. In fact, she may have provided an almost acceptable haircut for both Billy and Jimmy (maybe not). I think Mom said she actually had a little difficulty even recognizing Nancy, except for the clothes she wore. Her bangs (which Mom had styled as only mothers can) were drastically modified into a new style that Mom was quite unfamiliar with. Mom said it was more than weeks, perhaps more than a month before any noticeable improvement was achieved. I don't know if any of them maintained a long-standing relationship with her over the years, whether they were ever asked to provide references for her, but apparently their experience was memorable to them (and their mothers).

CHAPTER TWO

LIFE ON BOY SCOUT ROAD

MOVING FORWARD

Moving forward a bit; the next location where we lived was in a big old frame house way back off the road on Boy Scout Road, outside the city. Again, as was often the case in those days, it was a multi-family residence. I recall that the families were about the same as Jenkins Street (at least part of the time) and it's my story. So here goes. I actually do recall a few things of experience in my memory, and others that I was told. I will share some of both. First, I will share one that I was told:

ALICE LEARNING TO SHARE

It seems that Alice and I both had our baby beds in the same room, or at least very nearby, like adjoining rooms. Let's just say our beds were in the same room. Being a little, petite Southern girl, Alice would often very neatly drink part of the milk in her bottle, then carefully place the bottle under her pillow for later. Well, being the rather cute little boy that I was, with the appetite that I apparently had as a developing toddler, I could fairly quickly consume every drop of my bottle, then sometimes (but surely not always) throw my empty bottle out of my bed onto the floor. Alice, pretending to be napping, would then observe me as I skillfully managed to climb out of my baby bed, crawling and awkwardly walking toward her bed. I would then "pull-up" (stand), holding her bed with one hand; she would then watch while I reached under her pillow with the other hand, retrieving her bottle, turning it up and drinking it all. I would then return her empty bottle (probably quite carefully) under her pillow. After remaining silent for that entire time, Alice would now stand and rather loudly cry out, "Day, Day, Day, Day" (short for David, I suppose), as she would attempt to gently pat me on the head. I'm sure that was her intent, but after a few episodes, I was told I learned to stay out of range, though I am sure she wasn't attempting to hurt me.

During this time, I recall that Uncle Willie drove a van that was sort of a "store on wheels," mostly selling grocery items, but with some variety, probably including some clothing, bed linens, etc. I believe this was about the time when Uncle Bill became a bus driver for the City of Augusta. I recall that occasionally he would show us a blackjack or a small billy-club, for dealing with unruly passengers, but he always assured us that he never had to make use since his passengers were always so nice. I think my Dad, a former South Georgia "gentleman farmer," was learning about the carpentry trade. He always (quite humbly) said that he helped build Camp Gordon (later became Fort Gordon) and Parris Island (SC), a Marine base. Ladies were mostly moms and housewives back then.

ALICE AND ME AND ARMY WORMS

I do recall (from memory of experience), during the toddler stage when we were both walking pretty good, that Alice and I often walked around the yard, "bare-feet," holding hands. I'm not sure of the season, but I recall a time when these ugly old fuzzy worms would fall out of the trees around the house, and we had to watch where we stepped. I think some folks may have called them Army worms, but I don't know why. They didn't seem to bother us; they were just "creepy."

The Wood Pile

I'll share another episode that I was told of while we lived there. Mom said I was a REALLY GOOD kid, but I was pretty active sometimes. She shared that one day, while we were all outside, I climbed up a pile of wood that could best be described as scrap lumber. I don't know why the pile even existed, but it was a fairly large pile, and Mom became concerned when I had climbed up quite high, and although I recall always being a very obedient child, I either did not or felt that I could not come down when she directed me to do so. Perhaps I did not hear her clearly. Yes, that may very well be it or perhaps I didn't clearly understand her directive. Anyway, being the great Mom that she was (and the love and concern she felt for me, her only son), she began to climb up that pile of scrap lumber to get me (I'm sure it was an intended rescue and not a disciplinary action that she had in mind). Then (and I have regretted this for much of my life), things went awry. Mom stepped on a nail that protruded from an old piece of lumber. Since she was obviously in pain and since it was a rusty old nail, someone had to take her to University Hospital (which was not nearby) where she was given a shot for tetanus. I'm still sorry today, since I caused this, and believe me, back then, it was a big deal to find someone with both time availability and a vehicle who could (and would) stop what they were doing and drive someone to the hospital, stay with them until treatment was complete, while having someone else watch your kids until you returned. Thank God for relatives and friends like that!

The Indian Cave

I also remember that some of the older kids located what we called an Indian cave on the back of the property. I do recall this from my memory of experience, but I don't remember a lot about the cave. I have, however, wondered as an adult (especially since moving back to Augusta from Maryland in 1990) about the current status of that cave. I think that area today is generally a development of residential homes, and the cave may very likely no longer even exist.

A Real Barn Burner

I recall another incident that occurred while we lived on Boy Scout Road. It occurred during the night, and I only recall the story, not personal experience memory. As I recall the story, we had an old barn on the property, and my Dad (and others) likely had a cow and probably a mule that spent the night in the barn each night. For whatever cause (whether lightning, a lantern, someone's cigarette, etc.), a fire was discovered in the barn one night. I don't recall that anyone or any animal was harmed, but it was an anxious time, and I think the barn was destroyed in the fire. Dr. Bill or Jimmy may know more about this.

CHAPTER THREE

The Charlie O'Hara House

On Our Own

Moving on, I don't know how long we lived there, but the next location I recall was at the intersection of what we now call Davis Road at Scott Nixon Road (which did not even exist back then), not far from Poteet & Son Funeral Home. Each family had now sort of started to move out on their own. It was a rental of a free-standing small frame house. We always referred to it as the "Charlie O'Hara" house. A gentleman named Charlie O'Hara (he may well have been Irish) owned and ran a "general store" with fuel pumps, etc., near where First Baptist Church's campus is now located, where Jackson Road meets Walton Way Extension, and we rented from him. I remember that Dad then had a Model A Ford coupe with a rumble seat. If you don't know what a rumble seat is, ask me (if I am still around) or some other older adult since my story is already too lengthy for the substance I am providing, for me to interrupt and explain what a rumble seat is. You could try Googling "rumble seat," but don't expect too much from that, either. Anyway, since our family was growing, and later my younger sister, Martha Anne, was born while we lived there, we obviously needed a larger family vehicle, and Dad soon bought a large green four-door Dodge.

Some of Our Neighbors

Our closest neighbors were Aunt Katie and Uncle Paul Griffin, next door, and I believe they also rented from Charlie O'Hara. They weren't really related to us, but we called them Aunt and Uncle anyway. They had two teenage daughters, Katherine and Janelle. Across the road lived a black family. They were Fred and Ida Hester. They had two kids, a boy and a girl around the age of Nancy and me, Odell and Neurissa. If you are reading this, Neurissa's name may not be spelled correctly, but I don't think you would likely know the correct spelling anyway (and remember, it is my story). We spent a good bit of time with our neighbors. They were good friends. Fred was sort of a self-employed mobile lumber man. He also had a Ford Model A, a sedan, larger than Dad's coupe with the rumble seat. He could quickly remove one of his rear wheels, attach a pulley to his axle, then apply and adjust a long drive-belt, attached to another pulley to a large saw he would set-up and use to dress trees into various sizes of lumber; 2×4's, 2×6's, planks, etc. We were still far from "integration" in the south, which came much later, but we also had not learned about racial prejudice, especially racial hatred. These folks were our neighbors and our friends.

How She Became Martha Anne

I do have other stories of my memory experiences while we lived there, but I won't share a lot of them here. I mentioned that Martha Anne was born while we lived there. Nancy was attending Perrin school, which is no longer a school today. She rode the school bus, and through the bus ride and attending school, she really developed admiration for a girl a year older, named Martha Anne Parrish and her brother, "Buster" Parrish, who was about Nancy's age. Nearly every day, when Nancy returned home from school, she would put one of her dresses on her poor little brother, David, who was now about 2 1/2 years old, and he would have to play house with her. She had him be Martha Anne. Well, she was his "big" sister. Mom was pregnant with my younger sister, who would eventually be born on October 25, 1941 (WWII was well underway by then, but prior to Pearl Harbor and the US entry into it). The weather in the Augusta area always gets a little crisp in late October, and that is usually when Hallowe'en and the Augusta Fair both arrive. I recall that some other family members took Nancy and me to the Fair since Mom had just been admitted (first birth in a hospital) to University Hospital to give birth. Whoever took us to the Fair (likely Aunt Eleanor and Uncle Bill), then took us directly to the hospital to meet our new baby sister. Shortly after we arrived in Mom's room, they brought that new precious baby girl (God's special gift to our family) into the room. I quickly blurted out, "She's Martha Anne! I'm not gonna be Martha Anne anymore!" So-o-o!

CHAPTER FOUR

THE FIRST HOUSE DAD BUILT OR GRANDADDY'S GIFT

A HOUSE AND FIVE

Naturally, I do have more sharable memories of living at the Charlie O'Hara house, but I feel I must move forward. I may share more from there later. Grandaddy, William Robert Reeves, Mom's Daddy, owned quite a bit of land not too far from the "Charlie O'Hara" house along what was then referred to as Walton Way Extension, which, of course, today is known as Skinner Mill Road (progress in the USA). Grandaddy owned land on both sides of the road just as you begin going down a fairly long-descending hill to Rae's Creek (the same creek that runs through the Augusta National Golf Course, where the famed Masters is played each year) as you're headed toward Washington Road. Sometime around 1941, perhaps about the time Martha Anne was born, Grandaddy decided to give his six adult children a choice of two options: (1) they could receive $500 to use, however they chose or (2) they could elect to receive five acres of his land. Mom and her eldest sister, Aunt Janie, and Uncle Charlie Huffman chose the land; the rest took the five hundred dollars, which was considered quite a bit back then. They both built homes, so the Huffmans became our neighbors on one side, and Grandaddy and Dorothy and their son, Paul, who was about Nancy's age were on the other side. <u>Note</u>: At this writing, Paul, my uncle, and the last surviving sibling, who is retired from his electrical business, resides in Waynesboro, Georgia, with his wife, Sally.

Skinner Mill Road was still not paved at that time. It was in some parts sandy, but it was mostly clay, or what I refer to as sand-clay. We lived there for around three years, and they were all war-time years. Since they were war years, we often saw seemingly endless convoys of troops, trucks, jeeps, etc., moving down the road, sometimes all day long. They would often have an advance Jeep or motorcycle escort, well ahead of the convoy, and the rider would sometimes stop and talk with us kids for a while, and sometimes even accept a cool glass of water or iced tea.

The Huffmans were good neighbors, and we grew quite close to our cousins, which I mention in descending order of age: Charles, the eldest, who went by the name of Junior all of his life, Colden, who was about the same age as my sister, Nancy and Jimmy Holden, Vera, slightly older, but about the same age as Alice Reeves and me, and Marie, the baby, nearest in age to Martha Anne. Vera is her only surviving sibling at this writing. I will share more "David and Vera" stories, so continue reading, especially if you like fishing stories, and birthday stories.

SIMPLE, BUT SOMETIMES DANGEROUS

I will just offer a "shotgun" accounting of some of our interactions with our Huffman cousins. We often played with "simple" things, e.g., we might cut a tree limb, say about six feet long (perhaps sometimes strip the bark off), maybe tie a piece of string or small rope to the larger end, straddle the limb, pretend the limb was a horse (a white horse like the Lone Ranger's "Silver" if we stripped the bark off), and spend hours just running around, often competitively, either racing or some sort of attack. We often rolled metal barrel-hoops while guiding the hoop with a stick as it rolled. We would sometimes place ourselves crouched tightly inside of a truck tire or often even a smaller car tire, totally placing ourselves (our very lives, in fact) at the mercy of and trusting one of our cousins to roll the tire safely, which wasn't always the case. We made great use of that long descending hill that I mentioned earlier. Sometimes, a cousin might be rolling another in a tire down the hill, and the tire would accelerate to a speed where the "roller" cousin could no longer keep up, so it became a really exhilarating ride right up until you finally crashed into a ditch. We would also sometimes go into the woods at the rear of our homes, where it was fairly hilly. We would find a strong-looking sapling (of course you know that's an immature tree), several of us would bend it (always uphill) near to the ground, then a volunteer cousin would hold on (usually someone smaller). The others would then release the sapling tree; it would spring forward, and the volunteer would try and release the tree at the right time, thus go flying (downhill) through the air! We also liked to trick each other. One of the things was to dig a hole about 12"×12" and 12" deep. We then filled the hole with water, covered it with paper, and sprinkled pine straw or leaves over the paper. The trick then was to call a cousin over, so that they unknowingly stepped into the hole filled with water. I was on both ends of that trick several times. Unfortunately, Colden got me really good one Sunday morning, just before we were to leave for Sunday school, and I was dressed really cute and was wearing a brand-new pair of white shoes. I didn't get too many new shoes, and this may have been one of the few white pairs I ever had. Sunday was supposed to be off limits for these kinds of tricks, but although I loved him, Colden did not always play fair. We would also swing from large vines like Tarzan, and we made bows and arrows, slingshots, musical instruments from bamboo, etc.

Fishin' With Vera

Sometimes Vera and I would cut a couple of limbs, a little like we would for the horse stick above, but to be used as a fishing pole. We would then find a tin can and dig up a few earthworms for bait and head down the hill to the place where Rae's Creek crossed under the road. Unfortunately, even though we could always find a stick for a pole, some sort of string for a line, and maybe even rig some substitute for a cork, we never seemed to have a fish hook, so we would always just bend a straight pin, tie it to our string, and apply one of our worms. We would get bites, but we never caught any fish! We never totally figured it out, but we suspected it had something to do with fish hooks. We knew about fish hooks, but we never had any. We had fun fishing, though.

More Neighbors

At the bottom of the hill, really near Rae's Creek, we had some neighbors who were our friends. They were the Norris family. Their Dad was named Jamey, and Dad already knew him. The Mom was Mrs. Norris. I don't recall that I ever knew her name. A daughter was the oldest, and she was June. There were two sons: Sammy, who was near Nancy's age and Warren, who was around my age. I recall that when I visited with them, they had a pen in their backyard, and for some time, it contained a "mother" opossum (which we just call possums) and I think about four babies. I don't know why they had them, but they were fun to watch. That may be the only time I've ever seen baby possums. I've learned in my adult life that possums are often born dead in or alongside of roads. You've probably seen some yourself. A common kid's joke I learned later was the traditional question: "Why did the chicken cross the road?" However, the answer was no longer the traditional reply: "To get to the other side." Instead the answer was "To show a possum that it could be done!"

Vera's Fifth Birthday

Dad was working at the Augusta Arsenal (where the main campus is today for Augusta University), just off Walton Way. He worked nights much of the time. Though he and Mom were always real

Christians, these were tough times to get up and make it to Trinity-on-the-Hill United Methodist Church (UMC) on Monte Sano Avenue between Walton Way and Central Avenue. However, Aunt Margaret, Mom's youngest sister, only a few years older than Billy Holden and Junior Huffman, was given the job of counting heads, keeping up with all of us kids. We would load into the car, and Dad would always drive us to Church for Sunday school, then return later to pick us up.

Actually, this is where this story really begins. Sunday school had just ended. Trinity-on-the Hill was not yet a mega church, but it had grown a lot since my Grandaddy Reeves had been one of its founders (and also a founder of Pierce Memorial UMC on Jackson Road) years before, and there were lots of young families; therefore lots of kids. All of the children's classes would first meet in an assembly. Usually Mrs. Shields or Mrs. Battle would give a prayer and a brief devotion. We would pass the offering plate, sing one or two songs; one of them was usually "Jesus Loves Me," and another was almost always "This Is My Father's World," and I still love that song today. We would then go to our respective (age group) classes. There were many kids at the church (and you usually try not to have large children's classes because of "attention span issues" which even good kids have). So out of all of our other cousins, Vera and I were in a different class from the other cousins.

Perhaps the class that Vera and I attended was dismissed slightly later than the others that particular Sunday. At any rate, when Vera and I came out of our building and began walking toward Arsenal Avenue (runs parallel to Monte Sano along the rear of the church) where Dad would pull up to the curb (so we could all load up for the ride home). We saw that large green four-door Dodge I mentioned earlier. We saw Aunt Margaret hop into the car, and Dad pulled slowly away. I'm pretty sure Aunt Margaret must not have counted heads that Sunday because she was very smart, and if she had counted, we would not have been left behind.

What Now?

As she realized our situation, Vera became quite upset, crying, "They've left us, and it's my birthday!" I was still four years of age, and it was Vera's fifth birthday (and she was quite correct! It seemed apparent that we had been left). There may have been adults somewhere who had not yet gone into the Church Sanctuary, but for a four-year-old, I felt fairly confident that God would look after us, especially since we were just a couple of little kids (and we had just left Sunday school)! I tried to convince and calm Vera. I didn't try to find any adults to help. I took Vera's hand (or perhaps I was already holding it). Though just a little kid, I did know the area fairly well, so I told Vera that if we walked up Arsenal Avenue a few blocks, we would get to Walton Way (which was a main thoroughfare). Since I was just a little kid, I hadn't planned what we would do after we got there. We were well aware that we had both placed the few coins we had in the offering plate during Sunday School Assembly.

The Rescue

I have already discussed the phone situation in our society at that time, so I won't go there again, but I knew if we did find a phone, we had no phones at home to call. Well, I learned fairly early in life, that if we trust God, let Him take over whenever things look bad, and we do what we can while trusting Him, He does a real good job of solving bad problems. He did. When we got to Walton Way, there was a bus stop. Vera and I knew about buses, especially since Uncle Bill Holden was a bus driver. However, neither of us had ever ridden a bus before (and besides, we had no money). We met two really nice soldiers. Since they were wearing their khaki uniforms, we knew they were soldiers; otherwise, we may have assumed they were angels (and they could have been, I guess). They soon learned of our plight, and naturally, they learned that it was Vera's fifth birthday.

We trusted them. They had us board the bus with them. We never learned where they had planned to go, but we went with them downtown; the nice bus driver let us off at a bus stop nearest the Augusta Police Station. They stayed with us until they were sure we would be okay. All of the policemen we met (neither of us had ever been inside a police station before) were also really nice. I recall that one of Vera's relatives was a policeman, and when he saw us, he sort of took over. I still don't know how they got word to our parents, but they did. I think Dad came, so we were rescued, and we all lived happily ever after. As an adult, I still have a lot of respect and admiration for our military, police, firefighters, and other "first-responders." I don't recall any details, but I'm sure we later had a celebration for Vera's fifth birthday!

I remember well, that as Martha Anne became a toddler, she loved to pick Mom's flowers—all of them. I just thought I would throw that into this part of my writing.

I do have to share a few more stories from when we lived on (remember, we called it) Walton Way Extension:

Burned Hands

Dad always had chickens, etc., and he always had a· garden. One summer, some hot pepper plants that he had planted really produced. Many in the family liked to sprinkle some pepper vinegar on their greens, like turnips, and other country-type dishes during a meal. Since we had all of these peppers, Mom was "canning" them: putting some up in sealed jars, with vinegar. Recall that on the first line of this story above, I clearly stated that they were hot peppers. Mom's hands were badly burned from handling them, she had to see a doctor, she was in lots of pain, and she was even unable to perform many of her household duties for a short while.

Speaking of Burned Hands

This story involves that precious sister toddler, who quite willingly became Martha Anne, instead of me. She doesn't recall this event, but although she doesn't, I, her favorite big brother became her hero anyway, even if she doesn't remember. It's a shame that she doesn't recall it, but she was just a little kid. In those days, we did not yet have electricity. In cold weather, we had a "pot-bellied" stove (don't ask me why the name; 'twas something to do with the shape). We burned either or both wood and coal. The stove could become very hot, even red hot. My sweet little angelic sister was "toddling" around the house, and as she came near to that red hot stove, she suddenly lost her balance and was falling toward that stove. Her always protective big brother (who was now maybe four years of age), saw this, and quickly responded, pulling her gently, but quickly away from the stove, while his momentum continued leading him to the stove in her place. Apparently born with and blessed with good reflexes, he was able to then hold up his hands in front of him to catch his fall, so the palms of both hands were badly seared. Hey, it's okay. In the other story above, his Mom bravely survived, and he did, too.

The Night Visitor

I've mentioned a couple of times that Dad worked at the Augusta Arsenal, and these were WWII years. Dad's brother, Uncle Jimmy, would often drop in (sometimes in the middle of the night) to spend a night, a week, or longer. Our home wasn't huge, and he would sometimes just come in and always find room to join me in my bed. Well, one night (during the night), I felt a body breathe a sigh and turn over, shifting more weight onto me. It was enough to waken me, and I recall pushing on his back and saying something like "Uncle Jimmy, move over!" Well, I've also mentioned that Dad usually had chickens and maybe a cow or two. Early the next morning, Dad went out to milk his cow, and when he came back in, he said, "Something's going on! I saw some really large footprints in the barnyard, and the cow hardly had any milk this morning." I chimed in with a question, "Where is Uncle Jimmy? He wasn't in the bed with me when I woke up." Dad said, "Uncle Jimmy didn't come last night!" I quickly said, "Somebody did!" and I then shared my story. I have not mentioned this before, but practically during the entire time of WWII, some German prisoners were confined at the Augusta Arsenal. Occasionally one of them would somehow manage to escape. I suppose that it was only natural that following a successful escape into a strange country, they might need to drink lots of milk and possibly even need somewhere safe to get a little sleep. After Dad learned at work later, that there was an escape (aha! now knowing a bit more), I also realized that my visitor was quite a bit bigger frame than my Uncle Jimmy, and I recalled later that I heard no snoring, and Uncle Jimmy did! Hey, none of us were hurt, so it was a good story, I suppose. Before I forget, there are a few more memory small stories while living there, but they're not all clear to me:

My Secret Friend

Many young children go through a stage where they have a secret friend, so I suppose I was no different. My friend wasn't secret to the extent that I never spoke of him, but secret because no one ever saw him but me. His name was Nicodemus (John 3:1–12, John 7:50–53, and John 19:39, 40). Don't worry about the spelling. I looked it up. Nicodemus was tiny, and he lived on the "back-slope" of a clay ditch on our side of the road but slightly uphill from our driveway. He was usually available, and I always saw him in about the same location.

I don't really recall any specific conversations that we had. The mystery that troubles me a bit today, as I recollect my friend, is that I don't recall learning of the biblical Pharisee mentioned in the scriptures above until I was a lot older than the age of three or four. Perhaps I was even an adult. In Sunday school and Vacation Bible School, we often learned of biblical characters, but especially when younger than five, we didn't cover Pharisees named Nicodemus talking with Jesus. As you may recall, we were told of those like Mary, Joseph, Abraham, Moses, Samson, Jonah, etc., but no Nicodemus. I don't know where I got the name, but I did; maybe before I could even read, write, or spell. When we finally moved to our next home on Monte Sano Avenue, I left Nicodemus behind.

THE ECHO

This one is not so much a story, as it's just a somewhat bizarre memory. As I said before, Grandaddy owned land on both sides of the road. If you crossed the road and continued walking into the woods and fields, you soon arrived at Rae's Creek. This particular area of Rae's Creek was different from many other areas where it flows that I am familiar with. This area was not heavily wooded, as I recall, and it is the only area where much of the banks of the creek were mostly clay, instead of sandy, and with lots of slate. Actually, I don't recall a lot of slate areas elsewhere in the Augusta area. This feature may or may not have anything to do with the rest of this accounting, but we could stand on our side of the road, yell out a brief call, and ulti-mately, we would hear a resounding echo, virtually repeating our call, often numerous times. For us kids, this was a strange phenomenon, and we would do this fairly often, and (apparently for no particular reason), we would usually yell our call in the late afternoon, as we were approaching sundown (or sunset).

THE PLANE CRASH

This story is from memory, but I certainly do not have a full recall of all (or many) of the details. We would all spend a lot more time outside then than we seem to today. Perhaps this is because we had no air-conditioning (nor even electricity, as mentioned earlier), so we could be just as comfortable (or uncomfortable) outside as we might be inside. One evening, as dusk was approaching (that was what we called it when a day was turning into a night), most of the family was outside around the front of the house. There were other family there, too; perhaps Uncle Charlie Huffman from next door and maybe one of Dad's brothers. Suddenly, we all heard and saw a small plane across the road, which appeared to be struggling to stay in the air. Finally, we realized that it was going down, so Dad and a couple of the men grabbed a flashlight and ran toward the action. As they were crossing the road, running (they couldn't drive there), we all saw the plane crash into the tops of pine trees in the woods.

Well, unfortunately, I suppose, that is where the story ends for me. We witnessed the crash, but there was no explosion or fire. However, we kids were never told of any follow-up report. I don't know if the pilot was alone or if there were others. I don't know whether the pilot (or anyone else) was injured (or perhaps killed). I don't know if it was just better that the story end there for us, and anything else remain unsaid.

LEARNING TO DRIVE

I mentioned Aunt Margaret earlier regarding Vera's fifth birthday. She actually came and lived with us later, but at this writing, she was still living at Grandaddy's next door. She was anxious to learn to drive, and when she finally did, she became a very good driver. In this story, she wasn't quite there yet. As you came out of our front door and looked to your left, you would see Grandaddy's house, around 500 feet or 600 feet away. About 30 feet to 40 feet from our house, there was a bank sloping downward, around six feet, with a fairly steep grade into a mostly tree-less field. Our car was sitting in the yard, unlocked, and the keys were readily available. Dad may have been working some nights, as mentioned earlier, and he may have been at home sleeping.

A car with a clutch took some practice and experience, and automatic transmissions were still mostly on the drawing boards back then. Aunt Margaret successfully got the car started, overcame the clutch thing, and soon got the car moving. When she realized she was heading toward that downward embankment, she could not figure how to stop the car. I think I recall that she actually bailed out; the car continued down the bank, and for a short distance in the direction of Grandaddy's house, then choked down and came to a rather peaceful stop. After the excitement mellowed and the attempts of explanation by a really smart teen, it was discovered that no one, nor the car (it may have still been that large four-door green Dodge), had been injured or damaged. The only problem appeared to be the best way to get the car back to the right place. Dad took care of that, and no one was really upset except Grandaddy, and like most parents, his concern was mostly about how it could have been worse! It certainly could have! Before I forget, sometime while living near Grandaddy, we traded the large four-door green Dodge for a (sort of gray, I guess) 1935 Chevy sedan, which was still roomy.

God's Protection

Since Junior was older than me, we hardly ever played together, just him and me. Well, one day we were together, and we went in the back door of our house. I don't know why, but we headed toward Mom and Dad's bedroom, where we could hear Dad snoring. As usual, he was working nights. I followed Junior into the room. Dad was obviously sleeping very soundly. We watched, a bit amused for a while, observing a house fly that would fly near Dad's mouth as he snored, and we wondered if the fly might get into his mouth. He never did. Then, for some reason (I suppose it was mostly Junior's inquisitiveness), Junior slowly opened the drawer of the nightstand beside Dad's bed. He seemed pleased at what he found in the drawer; it was Dad's 38 caliber "police special" revolver. He removed it from the drawer and held it in his hand, admiring it. He saw that it was loaded. Then something very strange occurred. I'm certain that he had no intention of injuring me, but he pointed the pistol at me and said, "What if I pull the trigger?" He then pulled the trigger, and I think I heard the most meaningful, blessed "click" of my life. It misfired! This upset Junior. Perhaps he did not even plan to really pull the trigger, and he was so relieved to hear that click himself. He opened the drawer and carefully placed the revolver inside. We left the room (and the house), and Dad nor anyone else (except God) ever knew we were even there.

CHAPTER FIVE

603 Monte Sano Avenue

Back in Town

Throughout my life, I've had the numbers "603" several times. Some time in 1944, my parents decided to move back into town. There were some real advantages. The location they selected would have electricity, telephone availability (albeit a "party line"), city sewer, sidewalks, be nearer to Aunt Eleanor and Uncle Bill, who lived a block or so away on Oakland Drive, nearer to Uncle Willie and Aunt Montine, who lived just a few more blocks further, we would be nearer to Trinity-on-the-Hill UMC, and especially because we would be nearer to schools that we would be attending for a few years. As it turned out, we kids were delighted because we now had our very own local store a mere few steps away. More about Berry's Grocery later.

I have lots of memories of 603 Monte Sano since we lived there for around seven years: 1944 until 1951. I'll try not to bore readers with too many of them, but I may not be very successful. We were one of three homes on our block. If you stood in front of our house, Aunt Mary Huff, a widow and her son, "Fatty" Huff (he was a big guy) were to the left. She happened to be Uncle Bill Holden's Aunt, and his parents lived with her most of the time that we lived there. By the way, she was not related to us, but since our cousins, Billy and Jimmy, called her Aunt Mary Huff, we did, too! If you're still standing in front of our house while that was all being said, then I'll point out that our neighbors to the right, were the Swints. I think they were Melvin and Plura. They had a son, Charles, about the same age as Martha Anne, and a younger daughter.

COASTER, SKATES, AND FLIGHT

When we first moved there, we found a coaster under the house that someone had left behind. I think that's what it was called. At least that's what we called it. It was a wooden frame, a lot like a snow sled, except it had wheels instead of metal runners. It had two grips on the front that we could hold, steer, and pull down on to brake. So I will call it a coaster since it's my story. I don't recall what became of it, but we had it for quite a long time, and it would fly! While living there, we were somehow able to purchase the classic metal roller skates with metal wheels, a little leather strap to secure across the ankles, and, of course, the "key," for tightening or loosening the metal clamps up front near the toes. Most of Monte Sano sloped downward all the way from Walton Way to Wheeler Road, below our house. Our part of Monte Sano was an even steeper downhill slope, especially from about Oakland Drive. We could really fly on a bike, those skates, or that coaster! I reached a point where I felt I was a "purty good" skater. We always skated and rode the coaster on the concrete sidewalks. Someone between our house and Oakland Drive had a fairly vicious-looking bulldog, though I readily admit that he was always confined to his yard, and never interacted with us. However, one lovely day, I skated up the hill to Oakland Drive so that I could zoom back down. I saw the dog as I was going up, but I didn't give him another thought. Heading back downhill, I wasn't yet flying, but I was accelerating quite rapidly approaching flight! Most of the joints between the sections of sidewalk were a little wide, and the metal wheels made a distinct noise as they crossed each joint. As I continued gaining speed, going faster and faster, the sound became exactly like a rather large dog barking, and appeared to be getting closer and closer to my heels! I briefly thought, *That can't be a dog. It can't be that dog*! I turned to my left, attempting to look behind me (while still accelerating, perhaps by now to the flying stage). It happened that I was approaching a section of sidewalk which was slightly uneven, because of a tree root underneath or something. Since I was attempting to look behind me, I failed to make the necessary adjustment for the un-level difference in height of the sidewalk, and I went sprawling (not flying) through the air. God has always looked after me at times like this, so I was blessed to land quite abruptly on the grass located between the sidewalk and the curb of the street. It was a rough landing for a kid with short pants on, but thank God, I fell away from the sidewalk. When I got up, I didn't even look. I knew there was no dog.

Phone, Alley, New Street

Because of the closer proximity, we visited a lot with the Holdens and the Reeves, and they did likewise. By the way, this may be a good time to announce that we now had our very first "dial-up" telephone, which, of course was on a "party line." Coincidentally, our phone number was 37469 and Aunt Eleanor's up on Oakland Drive was 37467. Later in her life, Mom was never one to stay on a phone call any longer than necessary, but I suppose this was sort of a "new toy." Even though it never turned into a marathon, Mom and Aunt Eleanor would talk quite a bit and quite often, at least until the "new" wore off. I recall a few occasions when I might be at Aunt Eleanor's house, and she would be on the phone with Mom. I would say "goodbye," start the walk home, then when I arrived home, Mom would still be talking with Aunt Eleanor! Our section of Monte Sano (which was a concrete paved street) was a rather steep downgrade to a virtual dead-end at Berry's store, which was on Wheeler Road (which was still unpaved for several more years). Wheeler Road was very sandy. As Monte Sano ended at Wheeler, with a slight dog-leg to the left there was a narrow, concrete alley that provided access to many African-American homes. (Note: the term "African-American" did not actually exist back then.) This alley continued downhill the equivalent of around two to three blocks, then had a dead-end with three metal I-beam vertical barriers. There may be more about the alley later. Immediately to the left of the entrance to the alley was (and still is) the entrance to Westover Memorial Cemetery. Could be more about the cemetery, too. Fairly shortly after we moved there, the city made a new street, Hazel Street. It went from Monte Sano to Highland Avenue. It ran alongside Aunt Mary Huff's house, so she then lived on the corner. Folks soon built houses down both sides.

BERRY'S GROCERY

We liked Mr. and Mrs. Berry. We (kids) visited their store as often as we could. Things were a little different back then. They weren't butchers, but they usually had some hanging bananas and hanging sausages, which evidently required no refrigeration. I recall many occasions when I would be there around lunch-time, and workers would come in, have Mrs. Berry slice them up about a half-pound of ham or bologna, they'd buy a loaf of bread (ten cents), a small bottle of mustard and another of mayonnaise, so they were all set after buying a quart of Sankens, a large local dairy white or chocolate milk in a glass bottle. Coca-Cola provided coolers for displaying their Cokes. The cooler was a (naturally red) chest-type, which opened from the top, (often stayed open), had some mechanical cooling ability, as I recall, and the Coke products would stand in about 6"–8" of cold water. The cooler had a bottle opener attached for customers to remove their bottle caps. All bottled sodas had metal caps lined with cork. One of our favorite drink things (at home) was to chill a bottle of Coke, then punch a hole in the cap with an ice pick (instead of removing it). We then had to suck the soda from the bottle. Oh, before I forget; there was a "deposit charge" of two cents per (all glass back then) bottle. Sometimes we used this to our benefit. Americans are (and have been for a long time) a "throw-away" economy. We could always easily scout around Berry's store and pick up enough bottles (or find a few in the intended trash container) to return for credit totaling enough to purchase a pretty good supply of penny candy. I sort of got my start in life buying little brown paper bags full of penny candy and reselling that penny candy at school for three cents. I had lots of good customers.

DIXIE CUPS OF SHERBET

The Berrys had both mechanical refrigerators and freezers in the back rooms. Oh, I forgot to say that they also resided in the back, and we kids sometimes visited with them. Most delivery trucks (and many homes) still did not have mechanical refrigeration. When we first moved to Monte Sano, and for some time thereafter, we still had an "ice box." Both of my sisters and I loved ice cream products from the large local Sankens Dairy. One of our favorites was small "Dixie cups" of sherbet. Since delivery trucks did not yet have mechanical refrigeration, they relied on a sufficient supply of ice or "dry ice" (don't ask) to keep their cold merchandise as cold as possible while delivering. Most of the time, the sherbet delivered to Berry's store was partially thawed, therefore, partially melted. Naturally, upon receipt, Mr. Berry would then store it in his freezer in the back room. It would then re-freeze. So-o-o, most of the time, when we purchased a cup of sherbet, it would be creamy near the top and icy on the bottom. We loved it that way, and we would actually complain sometimes when it wasn't that way! One of the more common ways of eating the sherbet was that we would pull the tab on the paper lid, pull the lid off, fold it sort-of in half, and use this modification as a spoon to enjoy our sherbet.

THE FUNERAL

I mentioned that the Berrys lived in the rear of their store. This was not uncommon. We sometimes visited with them, not frequently, but occasionally. They had no small children like us. They did have an adult daughter, who apparently did not live with them, but she sometimes visited them. As I recall, they had a couple of small dogs, who stayed in the back. Let's guess that they were fox terriers or something similar. Apparently, they had these pups for many years. I guess they were getting old. One of them died, and we were invited to come to their backyard for the burial ceremony. I recall that I was fairly impressed with the seriousness of but the compassion that was displayed at the funeral. That may have been the first time I was ever sort of a "pall-bearer" and at the age of only five or six.

General Comments

During the approximate seven years that we lived at 603 Monte Sano Avenue (1944–1951), there were several significant events that I recall. Of course there were many others, but I mention some more memorable to me.

1. As mentioned before, our beloved nation was still deeply involved with WWII with both the Japanese and Hitler and his Nazis.
2. Back then, Augusta still had two newspapers: A. The *Augusta Chronicle* was the (day) daily paper, and is still in active publication today, but did finally change hands a few years ago from the Morris family to a large media organization. B. There was an evening paper called the *Augusta Herald*, which was later purchased by the Morris group, which owned the *Chronicle*, and after many years, they closed it down. C. Keep in mind, there was no TV (in Augusta) yet. The movie theatres would always show a "newsreel" along with their "coming attractions" and a cartoon. They especially emphasized WWII action in their "newsreels," and that was probably where we received much of our "war news." The *Chronicle* almost always had adults with paper routes (probably since they were delivered very early in the morning). The *Herald* had lots of young "paper boys," who might even yell out their headline, much like our TV news anchors today are always announcing "break-

ing news." They carried their papers in a large shoulder bag when walking, or sometimes riding a bike.

3. Yes, we had electrical power here, but still no air-conditioning, except hand-held fans, like a folded newspaper. Many evenings most of the family might sit outside, and while there, *the Herald*'s paper boy would often come by. Sometimes he would have "big" news, like a battle where many brave, young, American military boys died in a particular battle. This was how we learned of President Roosevelt's death, Babe Ruth's death, General MacArthur's statement "We shall return" after retreating, then later returning and becoming victorious in the Philipines. We learned of "D" Day, "V-J" Day, Ernie Pyle's death and the best news, when we were finally victorious and WWII was ended, and the rebuilding could begin.

4. Hank Williams died in the back seat of his Cadillac, while being driven to an event in Louisiana in the wee hours of the night. This was too late to make the morning *Chronicle*. The *Augusta Herald* had already gone to press and been delivered the evening before. I learned of his death in my classroom at William Robinson Elementary. I was one of a classroom full of crying kids (and their teacher), after someone came into the room and announced, "Hank Williams died last night." That shocking news of Hank's death was as big to us back then as the announcement of the death of Elvis was many years later. I clearly recall that especially the three deaths of President Roosevelt, Hank Williams, and Babe Ruth were events where I cried, and so did everyone around me.

5. Before I leave this side topic of memorable loss of life, I recall the death of another celeb, a great professional baseball player himself, named Lou Gherig. Besides being a great athlete, I think he may have set a record, back then, for the number of continuous games he played in, until a horrible disease finally overtook his body. They ultimately

named the disease after him. What a way to be remembered rather than for your physical accomplishments!

6. I suppose, while speaking of loss, I should cover non-celebs, and actually mention some in our lives, like friends and relatives. With little or no concern for having them in any particular order, here are a few:

A. Mom's Aunt Mary Reeves (her Dad's sister, who never married, and lived with his family the entire time I knew her) passed. She was sweet, not a big talker, read her Bible a lot. We have a picture of her holding her open Bible in her lap.

B. Grandaddy Reeves, Mom's Dad, who was a diabetic all or most of his life, first lost his sight, then later had dementia. When I was about eight or nine, my parents would let me spend a lot of weekends with him, especially after he was bedridden in his home on Skinner Mill Road. I would do whatever I could, or was asked to do, by an older black man named Chris, who was hired to "tend" to Grandaddy. Finally, the family reluctantly agreed to have him admitted to a care home in Keysville, Georgia, where he died. I suppose I was around ten years old then.

C. I guess when I was in about the third grade at William Robinson Elementary, a close friend, Dana Wade, hung himself in a closet with a belt. To this day, I never heard any reasons or suspected reasons, whether accidental, suicidal, etc. He seemed as normal as the rest of us kids. We were pretty close friends, and Dana never appeared to be worried or upset. At that age, I didn't know much, or ever even heard much about suicide, depression, etc.

William Robinson Elementary

We walked about ten blocks back and forth to school. Sister, Nancy, three years older, attended two to three years ahead of me, and for the balance of my time, Martha Anne, three years younger, attended three years behind me. To this day, even though I proudly attended the Academy of Richmond County High School, and later received my BS Industrial Management degree from Clemson A&M (later became Clemson University), I tend to value my elementary school days as the main foundation of my life. I attended with kids from some of the wealthiest families in Augusta, but we weren't normally that "class-conscious" back then. I am convinced that, for the most part, I was blessed to have some of the best teachers at any school in Augusta (or anywhere else). Mr. Gaskins was our principal, but ALL of my teachers, grades one through seven, were all ladies. Many were widows or were never married. Teaching was their proud profession, and it was a huge part of their lives!

When I began first grade in Ms. Sharon's class, I became aware that most of my classmates had attended kindergarten. Hey, at that age, I had never heard of kindergarten, much less spell it! At that time, it had been around for a while, but was not yet part of our school system, and still wasn't for several more years. I was "purty smart," so I caught up with them after a few weeks. Our class textbook was mostly *Dick and Jane* with their dog, spot and their kitty. Another educational biggie was called the Weekly Reader; perhaps it could be said that it was sort-of a kid's newspaper. We did not have an event called show-and-tell (as my kids did years later). There were radiators for heat in winter, but no air-conditioning system. Every morning, we had morning prayer; we said the Lord's Prayer (even though many of my classmates were Jewish), we stood, placed our hands over our hearts, faced the US flag [then representing forty-eight states (before Alaska and Hawaii)], and we all repeated the Pledge of Allegiance. This was before "Under God" was added years later (I think by President Eisenhower). I think that every year, a couple of guys from Coca-Cola came. They gave each of us a red Coca-Cola pencil and a twelve-inch wooden ruler, which stated the

"Golden Rule" printed on it. Back then, we really had blackboards on the wall, and we (or the teacher) wrote on them with white chalk (which is probably deemed unhealthy nowadays). We had erasers to remove chalk from the blackboards, and I seem to recall that one of the disciplinary events was to be told to go outside and clean the chalk dust from the erasers (by banging them onto a brick or concrete surface). Hey, I don't know this from experience! I don't recall that I ever had to clean erasers! The school population was growing. On our grounds, we had a Quonset hut, a metal round-domed structure that was erected while I was attending, and I think it was soon after WWII ended. I think it was only large enough for one class, and I don't recall that I ever had a class in it. I guess, for the most part, we still were taught the three R's: Readin', 'Ritin' and 'Rithmatic. I think we began early, maybe even first grade, having spelling bees. (I never learned how "bees" became part of the name of the event). This seemed to become a bit more important each year, and also more competitive. I (humbly) declare that I was a pretty good speller (but I'll give my teachers the credit and God the Glory for this apparent gift). Ms. Lard was my second grade teacher. I think it was my third grade teacher, Ms. Henry, who would divide us into about four teams, and each team would have a name. I guess (since I was probably one of her favorites), I would usually be made captain of one of the teams. We usually had bird names, and I would usually get the chance to pick the first bird name, so over time, our team would always be the Cardinals. I would usually also get to go first picking team members, and the Cardinals were the most frequent winners.

Augusta City-Wide Spelling Bee

I think around 1948 (or 1949) we had a competition of individuals at school from grades five through seven. I was in fifth grade. That competition went on for a big part of a school morning, and I was deemed the survivor, who was selected to represent William Robinson in a city/county-wide spelling bee. The event was held at Joseph R. Lamar Elementary, on Baker Avenue, I believe, across and down the street from Richmond Academy High School (for boys). There were what seemed like hundreds of fifth, sixth, and seventh grade students from all over. I think we had either two or three judges, who also took turns giving words to contestants. One of the judges was Ms. Emma Wilkinson, who was an English teacher from Tubman High School, which was then all girls, and Richmond Academy was ROTC military and was still all boys. I later learned that Ms. Emma had been a best friend of Neva Reeves (then deceased), Mom's Mother, and my Grandmother. Ms. Emma had taught my Mom at Tubman, and a few years later, when Tubman became a Middle School (when I was in eighth grade), she was <u>my</u> English teacher.

Continuing with the city-wide spelling bee, it proceeded for an entire morning. I spelled words I had never heard before and longer than any I had ever heard before. Even though there was continual pressure (and I was aware that it wasn't about me, but the fact that I was representing my school, William Robinson), I somehow remained amazingly calm. Finally, everyone had been eliminated, except for a sixth grade girl from Houghton Elementary and me. Well, Ms. Emma (or another judge) said "Well, there are only two of you remaining now. Congratulations! We know it has been a strenuous day, and we've had no breaks, so take a few minutes, and then we will resume."

AFTER THE BREAK

Well, until that announcement was made, I am confident that I probably could have continued correctly spelling long, complicated words that I was unfamiliar with (maybe even from a medical school text or a NASA handbook) for many more hours, at least for the rest of the day. Unfortunately, when the "break" announcement came, I literally fell apart, after being so cool, calm, and collected and feeling so invincible, much like the story of Elijah, the prophet, who was so brave, confident, then, after a life-threatening message received from Jezebel, wicked wife of the wicked King Ahab, 1 Kings 17:1–5, 18, and 19:1–14, this extremely brave Man of God became a whimpering coward, running for his very life, until God rescued him.

Reality hit me, I guess, and I suddenly realized the finality of this moment in time. I went to the rest room, nervously had a drink of water from the water fountain, and with knees knocking together, I re-entered the auditorium. So-o-o, lucky me! I was given the first word. It was, by far, the easiest, simplest word I had been given all day! The word was "sleeper." I don't normally stutter, but this is what came out: "s-l-e-p-p, no, wait! s-l-e-e," when I was then interrupted by a judge, who said, "Sorry, you cannot make a change here." The word "sleeper" was then given to the girl, who, naturally, spelled it correctly. I should be proud that I was the runner-up in the city spelling bee that year, and I guess I am glad, but I think I learned something that day (not that it could have made much difference, or that I could have done anything to achieve a different outcome). I think I learned that it's not important how confident you were before; what's important is how prepared are you <u>NOW</u> to proceed, at this new stage, which is different! Oh, she and I had our picture in the *Augusta Chronicle* newspaper. She was given a twenty-five dollar bond, and I was told, "Congratulations for coming in second."

RECESS AND GAMES

At recess, we played many different games, and we had an opportunity to mix with and compete with kids from the other grades. We played football, soft ball, king of the mountain, war horse, cops and robbers, and others. The girls played lots of hopscotch and jump rope. I was never outstanding, but I was not the last one chosen to be on a team, either. We had the usual playground equipment, too: swings, jungle gym, see-saws, a slide. We boys also played a lot of marbles. Oh, we had our favorite "shooters," and we had our own rules, like "slippance," "hunch," "do-over," "killer," etc. Some things were taboo in a regular game, e.g., no "hunching" and no "steelies" could be used for a shooter. Sometimes we played "chase" with marbles all the way home from school. You hardly ever see marbles any more. One year, when I was in about the sixth grade, it was decided for William Robinson to host a city-wide marble tournament. All of us guys, who each thought we were the best, anyway, felt sure that we would have a distinct advantage, since we would be playing on our home turf, so to speak. Well, long story short, most of us were some of the first to be eliminated, and even though marbles was definitely a boy's game, a girl won the tournament! This was one of our first hints of changes to come years later, like "Women's Lib!"

KID'S LIFE AT 603 MONTE SANO

I guess you could say that we were "latch-key" kids. Since we weren't little kids anymore, Mom began to work, first some part-time, like gift-wrapping in a department store downtown over the holidays, then soon establishing a career at Camp Gordon, soon to become Fort Gordon. So yes, we would usually come home to an empty house, but we never did the "latch-key" thing; at least we didn't lock ourselves in. Our house was rarely ever locked, even at night. Although our country had been heavily involved in WWII for around five years, it wasn't fought on our soil, and security never seemed an issue.

SALLY

Usually once a year, a nice man would come around with a brown and white pinto Shetland pony. Her name was Sally. She always had a nice saddle and a leather harness and reins. I think he usually brought Sally around in the spring or early summer. He would invite us kids to mount her (one at a time). He then took our picture. He would return later with our lovely black and white pictures of us individually mounted (quite elegantly) on Sally's back. Sometimes our parents would buy them, but more often they would like to, but being frugal (plus there were three of us), they would respectfully decline. Oh, I think he always had the current year printed on Sally's stirrups. Don't ask about them.

Young Love

When we first moved to Monte Sano, Nancy and I attended William Robinson Elementary, as I've said before, or will, if I haven't already. Martha Anne was only three, so no school yet. Mom wasn't working much yet, so they were able to spend some time together, for a couple of years, at least. When I earlier briefly mentioned some of our neighbors (I thought it was fairly brief), I mentioned the Swints and their son, Charles. Charles Swint, about the same age as Martha Anne, soon fell in love with that cute little blonde. They at least became best buds, and I think they were until they started to school.

Charles had a little difficulty with some words, and Martha Anne's name was one of those difficulties, but I don't think either of them cared. In those days, Martha Anne probably preferred sleeping as late as possible much more than she liked getting up early. On the other hand, it seemed that Charles was a fairly early riser. He would come up on the front porch, and I'm sure Mom knew he was there, but she would not hurriedly stop what she was doing to greet Charles at the door. Charles would stand on the porch, sometimes for quite some time and call "Boff-Ann," fairly repetitiously. Once Martha Anne "came to life" and arose, Charles would join them as soon as someone would finally let him in. Much of their time together, they would just stroll all around the yard, holding hands.

Runaway Couple

One time, and I don't recall exactly what triggered it, but both Martha Anne and Charles decided they would run away together. I think they even shared this decision with Mom or Nancy. As it turned out, they didn't get very far. Charles and "Boff-Ann" only got as far as the corner of Hazel Street, and I guess there were about three reasons: 1. At least at this point in their young lives, they had never been any farther on foot. 2. The corner was in their plans, but they hadn't planned further than that. 3. They were both really afraid to cross the street without someone older holding their hand. 4. Both

Moms had always stressed that they should never cross the street without someone older. I don't recall whether they had asked, when they made their announcement, but I guess neither Mom had time to run away with them that day, and Nancy and I weren't interested. I think, for some reason, we had one of those pictures of Charles sitting in the saddle on Sally, the Pinto Shetland pony.

DELEGATION OF CHORES

Since Nancy was the oldest kid, Mom trusted her to see that we kids all did our chores after she began to work. I loved Nancy, but she was great at scheduling, so that her chores usually seemed lighter in the rotation system. It seemed that her duties were often something that we had just done yesterday, like heavy cleaning, mopping, laundry, etc. Although she was left-handed, she seemed to be quite good at drying dishes, and she often assured me (and sometimes our little sister, Martha Anne) that I had a natural gift for washing dishes, cleaning the tub and the toilet. She bragged on me a lot! As I said above, I loved her, but since she was three years older than me, she did "boss" me some, and actually "bullied" me a bit, too. Nancy was tough! She could beat up most boys her age. I don't recall all details, but one day (probably a short time before we moved to Wrightsboro Road in 1951), when she was "bullying" me, actually chasing me, for some reason, I suddenly "stood my ground," and in a few moments, I realized that I was chasing her, and she was running from me! So she still delegated, but no more "bullying."

GARDEN, HOLES, AND THE TREE

I tried gardening some. Mom and Dad showed me about saving the eyes of a potato and planting them. Well, the spot I picked for planting was shady most of the day, but in spite of that, my potato plants did come up, and later on, I actually had some potatoes form on the roots. That was about the extent of my gardening, though, but we did help Dad with his garden. We hoed the weeds out, picked peas, shelled some, etc. I think we kids really enjoyed digging! I only remember it as being one time, but somehow, I guess I either volunteered (or submitted) for this one. We dug a hole. I got in, and Nancy and Martha Anne filled the hole with dirt, only leaving my head exposed. I was found that way when Mom came home from work that day.

A few times, we dug some really large holes, larger than a gravesite in a cemetery. They would probably be at least four feet wide, eight or ten feet long, and maybe six to eight feet deep. We would usually slope the floor a bit on one end, but it was still challenging to get out. We originally had a secured rope hanging into the hole, but later we built a rather primitive ladder from some of Dad's scrap lumber. It was always pretty nice and cool in the hole, even in hot summer. Our lot was pretty sandy, so we could really dig. We had not learned about "cave-ins" or any danger or any reasons to fear. God knew, so He protected us from our ignorance.

In the front yard, we had an old China Berry tree. It was easy to climb, so we spent a good bit of time in it. As I said, it was old, so, one day I was sort of reclining on my back, lying on a rather large limb, when the limb decided to break and fall to the ground. It broke just above where my waist-line was as I lay there, so I was suddenly doing a "balancing act" on the remaining part of the limb that did not break off, until I could finally sit up, and grab another limb above me! Hey, we just didn't know about all of this dangerous stuff!

NANCY'S BUTTERMILK ACCIDENT

One day, before leaving for work, Mom left some money with Nancy, with instructions to go to Berry's store and buy a half-gallon of milk. Nancy did. Alice was visiting with us. When Mom got home, she realized that the (glass) bottle of milk was buttermilk. No problem; Berry's was still open. Although the sun had set and darkness was quickly approaching, Nancy took the bottle of buttermilk, and she and Alice went skipping across Monte Sano to the other side to make the exchange. Mostly because of the downhill course of Monte Sano, the concrete curb became increasingly higher as the street neared its dead-end at Wheeler Road at Berry's store. As they skipped over the curb, the step up caused Nancy to fall! She fell across the grassy area and landed (along with that glass half-gallon bottle of buttermilk) on the concrete sidewalk. She sort of fell on the buttermilk. The glass bottle shattered. Her forearm was badly cut. Well, Nancy got up, and she and Alice calmly crossed the street and returned home. Naturally, she was covered with blood and buttermilk! Mom cleaned her up a bit, and soon realized that she had a serious cut on her forearm that would require stitches. This was now an emergency situation, and it was soon decided that only Mom and Nancy would go to the University Hospital Emergency Room. The word came back to us that Nancy remained calm the entire time, while waiting, but Mom was hysterical most of the time there! We got more milk the next day, but not that night. Nancy healed well, but she carried that scar on her forearm for the rest of her life.

Do Not Kick Pin Cushions with Bare Feet

Nancy was rather good at coming up with ideas that I would never think to do! Mom had a "pin-cushion" doll. This was a quite pretty china or porcelain doll from about the waist up, (around 3" high), and her torso was mounted on a pin cushion 3"–4" diameter, say 3" high, made to look like the doll's fancy dress. As I've mentioned (or I will) in the summer, we kids were almost always barefoot. While Mom was at work, Nancy decided it would be nice to play with this pretty "pin-cushion" doll. After some time, she then decided it might be enjoyable to take her outside, so she did. After just holding her, which was a little boring for Nancy, she began tossing her into the air and catching her. Well, with one of the tosses, she was unable to catch the doll, and it fell onto the grassy lawn. This seemed to inspire Nancy to another level. She was curious to see how well and perhaps how far she could kick this doll. We didn't play soccer back then and didn't even know about it, but I will always believe that Nancy could have been pretty good, perhaps even a soccer star! Seriously, I was (sort-of) impressed at how well she moved and manipulated that "pin-cushion" doll around the yard, and surprisingly, it seemed no worse for wear! When she'd had enough, she picked the doll up and returned it to the location where Mom kept it. A day or so later, when Nancy was planning to put shoes on her feet, she felt something toward the front of her right big toe. She was left-handed, but she kicked with her right foot. When she enlisted Mom's help, it was discovered that part of a needle was embedded in Nancy's big toe. Apparently, the needle had somehow broken as it penetrated Nancy's toe, and she was so involved in her new kicking game that she had felt no pain! Mom wondered how in the world Nancy had part of a needle stuck in her big toe, and also that she didn't know it. I don't recall that Mom figured it out, so she never knew until Nancy eventually shared the story with her much later.

BIKING

I received a 24" bike one year, probably around age seven or eight. It was red. Nancy nor Martha Anne ever had a bike. I'm sorry about that. Alice had a smaller bike, about a 20". I recall that it was blue. Naturally, hers was a "girl's" bike. Occasionally, Alice's bike would wind up at our house. Sometimes she might come over on it and go home some other way. Sometimes Nancy might ride it home, perhaps after spending a night with Alice. One day, at Alice's house, Nancy had an accident. I think we may have been taking turns riding the bike. While Nancy was riding, she came riding up to the rather large flight of the back steps. Of course, we were all usually barefoot (which is not a great idea when riding a bike). Nancy's plan was to approach the steps, lift a foot off of a pedal, and place the foot onto the lower step, bringing the bike to a stop. I'm sure we had done this many times before, but for whatever reason, Nancy's aim was a little off. Her foot attempted to go under the step. The front edge of the step (which I will call the "bullnose") ripped Nancy's large toenail from her foot.

I enjoyed my bike. I sometimes rode it to school, but we walked much more. With a clothespin, I would sometimes clip a piece of cardboard onto a rear fender brace, so I had a pretty good engine-type noise. I would remove the chain, clean it in kerosene, put it back on the sprocket, and lubricate it with oil. I would sometimes adjust the handlebars into various positions. I would occasionally remove the wheels, change a tube, tighten the spokes, etc. I had a basket on the front sometimes, and found it useful, but it wasn't always convenient to have it mounted on the handlebars, so I removed it a lot. I would occasionally mount a pinwheel to the handlebars, just to see it whirl faster and faster as I rode faster and faster. I learned to balance the bike while standing still. I learned to ride "Look, Mom; no hands!" I could also sit on the handlebars, facing the rear of the bike, place my feet on the pedals and ride backwards. At the time I was pretty sure I would grow up and become a trick rider, or at least a mechanic. Neither happened, but I enjoyed that little old bike for many years. I was twelve when we moved to Wrightsboro Road. I took it with me, and I enjoyed it there until I learned to drive and discovered girls.

BALLERINAS

We were poor, I guess, but we didn't know it, and things were getting better. Mom arranged for both Nancy and Martha Anne to be enrolled in ballerina classes. We have pictures of them somewhere in their tutus. I can't recall that I ever saw them perform, but I am sure they were both quite agile, graceful and talented! Their tutus were fashioned and custom made by our rear neighbor, Mrs. Tantillo, who actually resided on Hazel Street. More about her later.

THE COAL TRUCK

One Saturday, while some of the family were sitting on the front porch, we were given a bit of excitement. The same company, using the same trucks, would sell large blocks of ice for people's ice boxes (non-mechanical refrigerators) in summer and deliver coal in fall and winter. We heard a truck, which turned out to be a coal truck, coming down Monte Sano. The driver was rapidly honking his horn! He was "panicly" (a word I sort-of made up for this story) waving his left arm out the driver's side window, yelling in a loud voice, "Help! Help! I can't stop! I don't have no brakes!"

My Dad was always prepared to respond quickly to an emergency. Although there wasn't much we could do, several of us quickly headed for the family car, and we were on our way to assist as much as possible. We could see that the driver had skillfully made the zig-zag quick left move and entered the (downhill) alley that I have mentioned a few times previously. The concrete curbs were 2'–3' high. We could see that he was going quite fast for a coal truck, and he was deliberately steering first left, then right, banging into the curbs (almost walls) in an effort to slow the truck down as much as possible. Meanwhile, he was literally tossing heaps of coal onto the alley. He made it to the dead-end, where he met with the steel "I-beams" standing vertically at the end of the alley, anchored securely into the ground. We saw his truck meet the barricade, literally go airborne, then landing on the passenger's side of the coal truck! The driver was both tough and very blessed! He crawled out of the driver's window, which was already open, shouting, "Hey, I'm okay! I just banged up one arm a little bit!" Well, that was the excitement, I guess. Dad and others hurried over to help him climb down. The entertaining part, at least to me, was that many of the black ladies who resided just off of the alley, came running out, grabbed their "dress-tail" (the hem area of their dress), creating a sort-of "open-sack" creation. They appeared to not even notice the driver's recent or current activities, as they hurriedly (and competitively) ran around picking up (free) coal, many with some help from their kids. I'm sure this was an exciting time for them. It was coal, not manna from Heaven, but surely it was a "gift from God!"! Since one of my jobs at home was to bring in buckets of coal (yes, we had coal buckets), vividly recalling how heavy a bucket of coal could be, I was quite impressed at how much coal they could accumulate and still walk, though walking in a slightly different way!

Tantillas

I mentioned earlier, albeit briefly, that Hazel Street was developed and constructed after we moved to Monte Sano. A really nice, classy, single guy purchased a new home on Hazel, which was immediately behind Aunt Mary (and Fatty) Huff, our next-door neighbors. His name was August Tantilla. He went by his nickname, Augie. He was Italian-born; he had previously served in the US Army, chose Augusta as his home, and he owned a "meat market" downtown. Shortly after purchasing his new home, Augie's Dad passed away in Italy, so he brought his recently widowed Mom to the US to live with him.

We soon came to love them both. Mrs. Tantilla spoke no English. She always wore black, even past the usual time I considered it to be for mourning the death of her husband of many years. She was an excellent seamstress, as I mentioned above. Although I assume that she was a devout Catholic, she was not quite sure of some US customs, even our Christmas customs. Even though Augie bought and mounted a "cut" Christmas tree (not a "live" tree with roots), when Christmas had passed, she insisted that Augie plant it in the front yard near their front entrance. The tree did not live. She apparently was a very good Italian cook. After both Martha Anne and I were recovering from a bout with the flu, when she learned of it, she baked some Italian cookies for us. I am sure that they were absolutely delicious, and we expressed our sincere gratitude, but although we attempted to bite them for several days, we were never quite successful. We were probably supposed to dunk them in something, perhaps coffee, hot tea, or milk. They looked great, though!

Language Barriers

We kids tried to teach Mrs. Tantilla some English, and she attempted to teach us Italian in return. It was a commendable plan, but with less than dramatic results! I have learned as an adult that Italian is much like Spanish, which may have now become the national language of the USA, as some of you may be reading this several years after I have written it. We learned that water was "aqua" or "agua," milk was "latta," toilet was "chessa," and we sort-of learned to count: ona, doce, trey, etc. The best I ever did was to ask for a glass of water: "Ere wall-ya ona bequila Aqua." Not only was the program less than successful; Dad never even knowingly participated. Dad was working mostly "night shift" work, so since Mom was now working and we kids were enrolled in school, he was often "home alone" for part of the day. Occasionally, Mrs. Tantillo would need some item that she could not locate in Augie's inventory of tools, even sometimes food, etc. Since we were the neighbors she knew best (and she knew we loved her), she would naturally come to our house to see if we could help. When she inquired if she could borrow an "Agos," Dad didn't have any idea that she wanted to borrow an egg! When she wanted to work in her yard (and she was always very active and busy), she asked Dad for a "chop chop." He tried to first give her a meat cleaver, then his hatchet, next his axe, before she finally spotted his hoe. They gradually learned to communicate a bit, but it wasn't easy!

AUGIE AND DOLLY

Augie, born in Italy, became quite Americanized while and after serving his (new) country in the US Army. He had become a successful business owner of a meat market. He was also a handsome, eligible bachelor. Dolly's parents were considered upper middle-income, I suppose, quite respected in business and social circles in Augusta. Augie and Dolly soon became a couple. They became engaged, then had an elegant, beautiful Catholic wedding. We kids did not attend, but our parents did, and they were both impressed. Dolly was a beautiful bride, and they were a seemingly perfect couple.

CRIMINAL DISASTER

One evening, a few months after the wedding, when business was quiet, and as closing time was approaching, Augie heard the bell tinkle that he had attached to the entry door, so that he could hear when someone entered. He stepped out of the rear, where he was cleaning, and saw that three people were coming in the door together. There were two men and a woman. He greeted them. They looked into the meat showcase display. One of them gave his order to Augie. While Augie was bent over, gathering the meat products, with his head partly in the meat case, one of the men quickly stepped around the meat case, and with a large pistol in his hand, he announced to Augie that this was a "stick-up," and they wanted all of his cash. Sort of as a reflex motion, Augie quickly grabbed a long link of sausage, backed out of the meat case, spun around, hitting the assailant in the face. Though he was startled and had not completely recovered, the man began to pull the trigger, and fired several shots into Augie's chest and abdomen. As Augie began to slump to the floor, all three people ran for the door, rushed to their vehicle, and sped away.

Within a very short time, a customer saw Augie's plight, notified authorities, who quickly responded. Though badly wounded, with considerable loss of blood, Augie somehow survived. He was admitted to the University Hospital, underwent surgery, and after several days, all were amazed at how well he seemed to be recovering. After several days, someone on the medical staff felt that it would be good for Augie to now get up and walk down the hallway of the hospital. With some assistance, he did. Soon after returning to his bed, his condition seemed to worsen. He did not survive the night. He was experiencing serious internal bleeding from his wound, which was detected too late to save him. Dollie Tantilla, the beautiful, deliriously excited, and happy recent new bride was now a widow. I was shocked to learn of his death the next morning while at school.

Tantilla Prologue

My parents then attended the funeral service in that same beautiful Catholic cathedral that had housed the wedding only a short time before. I think I was in about the fourth grade. This tragedy touched many lives, including our family. It was learned that the criminals had rigged an electric charge to the vehicle, somehow, so that if someone, say a suspicious police officer, should approach them, maybe touch the door, it could be activated to deliver an unsuspected electrical shock, thereby giving them precious time to get away. Apparently, they had an opportunity to test this out. The day after shooting Augie, there was a news report that they had been stopped for speeding near the Georgia and Florida state lines. The police officer approached their vehicle. They were unresponsive when he requested license and registration. The policeman first knocked on the driver's door glass, then grabbed the door handle. They activated the electrical setup, the officer did receive a brief electrical shock, and they did manage to quickly speed away before he could completely recover. It was too late. Now the authorities had a more distinct description of the vehicle and the occupants. They were apprehended in Florida within days, and justice was served. However, Mrs. Tantilla, who had lost her lifetime partner, then came to a strange country, new language, new customs, had now lost her son to selfish violence, and Dolly, Augie's beautiful bride, was still a widow.

Lots More

There is so much more about the neighborhood, church, school, etc. while we lived on Monte Sano, but I can't make this writing all about this phase of life here. I'll sincerely try to get back to it another time. The following are just a few other topics I would love to have magnified in more detail:

1. Westover Memorial is a beautiful cemetery. We kids thought it was our private playground. We played there a lot, roll-

ing down the hills, etc., never harming any gravesites. The swans were still at the goldfish pond; that area was still unfenced.

2. Nancy and I did quite a bit of babysitting in the neighborhood. I confess that it was mostly Nancy's business, and I was blessed to fill in for her when she was "booked up" or scheduled otherwise.

3. I was a "school crossing" guard at school. We directed traffic at intersections. We also raised the flag each morning, and lowered it and re-folded it each afternoon. We wore a red belt, all one piece that was around our waist and crossed over one shoulder. This usually made me and other crossing guards slightly late to "home room," but that was all okay.

4. I was a cub scout, probably for two to three years. Mrs. Harmon was always my "Den Mother." There were probably about eight to ten of us in her "pack." Lots of other cubs were classmates all the way through high school. Her son, Cornelius, was one of my best friends. We called him Ginny (hard G). Other cubs were Bill Kuhlke, Milton Burroughs, Cobbie Ware, Henry Marks, Bobby Anderson, Larry Puckett, Teasley Harris, Lamar "Skeeter" Tabb, Lou Saul, A. J. Furst, and others. Those were great times! I always felt Mr. Harmon, Corneliuss' Dad, looked like General (and later President) Eisenhower, better known as "Ike."

5. One of the families Nancy and I would baby-sit for were the Peskoes, who lived just a few houses away on Hazel Street. Stephen (or "Stevie") had a Mallard duck for a pet that he had acquired when it was just a duckling. He also had a baby brother. The Peskoes were Jewish. The grandparents built a house on Monte Sano, almost backed up to Stevie's house. His grandparents were older, of a more conservative Jewish faith, (which does not accept Jesus as the Messiah, Son of God), so therefore, no celebrations of Christmas or Easter. Stevie's family would have a Christmas tree (and

they celebrated Easter), always near the front door. When his Mom knew one or both of the grandparents were coming over, she would hurriedly slip the entire tree into the "guest" closet at the front door, and she did the same for any Easter artifacts.

6. We had the sweetest black lady, named Laura, who would help Mom keep up with the housework (that us kids couldn't or wouldn't do) once Mom began working. Laura was classy. We respected her; I'd say we came to love her. We were never confronted with any "racial" issues.

7. At church, attending Trinity-on-the-Hill Methodist, I think the first pastor I recall was Reverend Ellizer. We had the same janitor (today referred to as custodians) all through my childhood years, and clearly into my early teens. His name was Mr. Charlie Shaw. On September 28, 1947, I was given a Bible from Sunday school. Although it was extremely close to my ninth birthday on September 26, I think it was given because I was "sort-of" growing up, and was then moving up to the third grade Sunday school class. I still have that Bible.

8. Many cars would back up Monte Sano (because "reverse" was the lowest gear).

9. Sometime while we lived there, we upgraded to (probably the newest car we'd had) a blue 1947 four-door Chevy, probably around 1949. A few years later, after we had moved to Wrightsboro Road, I learned to drive in that car, with most of my driver training with Dad on Columbia Road, while it was still unpaved. Dad was a very good driving teacher.

10. We had lots of company visiting. Quite often, some of them stayed for months. Uncle Kemp, Aunt Lillian (Dad's sister), and Elaine were with us for quite a while when she was a baby. Sometimes eating sand, stating that she was feeding her earthworms, and she would sing, "Calledonia, what makes your big head so hard?" One of Dad's brothers, Delmar (our Uncle Dick) died in South Georgia

while we lived there, and his widow, Aunt Faye, Caroline (a little older than Nancy), Bo (a little younger than me), and Marilyn Sue (who was still a baby) lived with us for some time. Others did, too. At this writing, Bo is the only remaining sibling.

11. First Love

Speaking of Aunt Lillian and Uncle Kemp, shortly after they were married (after Uncle Kemp had just gotten out of the Navy), they lived in Savannah, Georgia. Soon after we moved to Monte Sano, but before I started first grade, Nancy and I rode the train to visit with them. In those days, Augusta had a fairly large train station and several trains ran out of there. One was named Nancy Hanks. We rode one named Little Nancy. While we were visiting, I met my first love. Her name was Ann Burkhalter, and she was as cute as a new kitten. Although I had not began school and was just learning to write, we corresponded for a while. Maybe more about Ann if and when I write about college days at Clemson. Maybe not. Anyway, we're a long ways from writing about that era.

12. Second Love

When I started to school that fall at William Robinson, I met my second love. Her name was Rebecca "Becky" Towell. We had many cute girls in our class, but Becky was obviously the prettiest of all. I fell in love with her, along with most of the other guys, but in this case, I never told her how I felt. I guess I loved her from a distance. I discovered girls and dated many, but I never asked Becky for a date. Years later, when Charlie Brown expressed his love for the "little red-headed girl," I could easily relate to his feelings.

13. As I must leave this era of my childhood, I know I should share the story about the hallway. Mom loved the location, but like lots of other wives and mothers, she didn't love everything about the house. It had a central hallway. She requested that Dad do something for a while. Not that she

was impatient, but I guess because she was ready for some progress. One evening, while Dad was working nights, she gave all of us kids a hammer, and we demolished the hallway walls. Mom was no architect or construction engineer, but like me, God has always looked after her! Thank God! It was not a "bearing" wall! (This is the name of any wall which has the responsibility to hold the rest of the house up, like the roof and stuff, and is not just there for looks.) After Dad recovered from what he found when he came home, he adjusted, took over, placed new partitions (fancy name for a wall) in just the right places, installed beautiful maple hardwood floors in part of the house, and we lived there happily ever after (until we moved years later).

14. What a shock!

    We had one bathroom. It had one hanging ceiling light. The hand sink was porcelain on metal. The light fixture had a short in it. Nancy and I discovered that if we touched the light switch and had our other hand on the sink, we could receive a pretty good jolt of current. When we finally shared this with Mom and Dad, it was repaired, so we lost our "kicker."

15. When we made our move to Wrightsboro Road, our family (and most others) still did not have a television (TV) set. Augustans would still go downtown on Broad Street just to watch the screen of a TV in a storefront from the sidewalk out front. Atlanta had TV for several years, and Augusta was probably working on and close to having their first TV station.

16. Oh! We couldn't afford a moving van company, and they did not yet have U-Haul, Hertz and Budget rental trucks yet, so we moved all of our stuff to Wrightsboro Road in Uncle Willie's dump truck since he had recently gone into the garbage pickup business. Sure, the bed of a dump truck is pretty high up. That just made the move a little more interesting.

Leaving Monte Sano

Like the rest of my family, I'm sure, I did have some mixed emotions approaching the move from Monte Sano. I had just finished the seventh grade of elementary school. I was twelve years old, and I had lived in this home with my family for about seven years, which was more than half of my life here on planet earth. I believe I truly enjoyed being a kid! Was it a perfect childhood? I could see a little of my life in the distant future. I think I no longer wanted to be a cowboy when I grew up. Perhaps I no longer even yearned to be a fireman or a farmer (since I saw how much some farmers had to sweat in their work). I think I realized that I would probably be a teen in a short time, perhaps before I was completely ready. I thought a little about college, and I was aware that so far, none of my Gibbs generation had attended, much less graduated from college. Only Billy (Dr. Bill) and Jimmy Holden had attended college on Mom's side of the family. I was aware that life would be different on Wrightsboro Road, with new opportunities. I was beginning to learn that this is what life is all about. It offers us opportunities, and there are many ways that we might respond. Personally, I've come to believe that it is more important to look forward to the future than to look back to the past. However, the past should be remembered, but with the realization that it is something that we have done, a place where we have been, and hopefully, we are able to see a few accomplishments that we have made, but knowing that it _is_ the past, whereas, the future is yet to be lived. That is an exciting thought, even for me today, in the latter years of my life. I now recall sharing the story of my roller-skating with you. Recall what occurred when I looked back at the wrong time while I was moving forward? Although I have a lot more I'd love to say about living there, I know I must move on. I'll hope to soon begin another short story (almost a novel) about life on Wrightsboro Road and the rest of my life.

ABOUT THE AUTHOR

Eldridge David "Dave" Gibbs has been around for a long time. Over the years, he has written quite a few poems. Some were written at the request of others. When requested, he always replies that he must be inspired. Although he has written poems and similar items, this is his first attempt to write a book. He shares that he was inspired to do so. He recommends that we all should consider such an undertaking, regardless of our writing abilities or experience. He is a native of Augusta, Georgia, a city well-known for the Masters annual golf tournament. Following graduation from the Academy of Richmond County high school, then Clemson in South Carolina, and after serving almost eight years in the Army Reserves, he was recruited into restaurant management while living in Atlanta by Marriott. Thus he became a resident of Maryland for the next twenty seven years. He and his wife, Deanna returned to the Augusta area in 1990 and reside there today.

CPSIA information can be obtained
at www.ICGtesting.com
Printed in the USA
LVHW032337210520
656258LV00003B/775